MYTHICAL CREATURES

# Vampires

## Charlotte Guillain

**www.raintreepublishers.co.uk**
Visit our website to find out
more information about
Raintree books.

**To order:**
☎ Phone 0845 6044371
▤ Fax +44 (0) 1865 312263
⌨ Email myorders@raintreepublishers.co.uk

Customers from outside the UK please telephone +44 1865 312262

Edited by Adrian Vigliano, Rebecca Rissman,
  and Nancy Dickmann
Designed by Joanna Hinton Malivoire
Levelling by Jeanne Clidas
Original illustrations by Christian Slade
Original illustrations © Capstone Global Library
Picture research by Elizabeth Alexander
Production by Victoria Fitzgerald
Originated by Capstone Global Library
Printed and bound in China by CTPS

ISBN 978 1 4062 1646 2  (hardback)
14 13 12 11 10
10 9 8 7 6 5 4 3 2 1

**British Library Cataloguing in Publication Data**
Guillain, Charlotte.
Vampires. -- (Mythical creatures)
398.4′5-dc22
A full catalogue record for this book is available from
the British Library.

**Acknowledgements**
We would like to thank the following for permission
to reproduce photographs: Alamy pp. **8** (© Pictorial
Press Ltd), **14** (© Jack Carey), **16** (© Ariadne Van
Zandbergen), **17** (© Steven Poe), **23** (© imagebroker),
**25** (© imagebroker); © Austen Zaleski p. **11**; Corbis
pp. **10** (© Michael & Patricia Fogden), **22** (© Mike
Grandmaison); Getty Images pp. **9** (Scott Mansfield/
Photographer's Choice), **21** (Karen Moskowitz/
Stone+), **24** (Hulton Archive); iStockphoto p. **13**
bottom (© oana vinatoru); Photolibrary pp. **19**
(Caroline Penn/Imagestate), **28** (Nick Gordon/OSF);
© Stephanie Hu p. **20**; The Kobal Collection p. **29**
(Maverick Films).

Every effort has been made to contact copyright
holders of material reproduced in this book. Any
omissions will be rectified in subsequent printings if
notice is given to the publisher.

**Disclaimer**
All the Internet addresses (URLs) given in this book
were valid at the time of going to press. However, due
to the dynamic nature of the Internet, some addresses
may have changed, or sites may have changed or
ceased to exist since publication. While the author and
publisher regret any inconvenience this may cause
readers, no responsibility for any such changes can be
accepted by either the author or the publisher.

Some words are shown in bold, **like this.** You can find
out what they mean by looking in the glossary.

# Contents

# What is a mythical creature?

A **myth** is a story people tell over many years. Many of these stories are about **mythical** creatures. But are the creatures real? People tell stories of unicorns. Do you think they are real?

4

Have you ever heard stories about werewolves? Do you think they really exist?

# What is a vampire?

People around the world have been scared of vampires for hundreds of years. Many of these creatures look like humans. Stories say vampires come out at night and suck human blood.

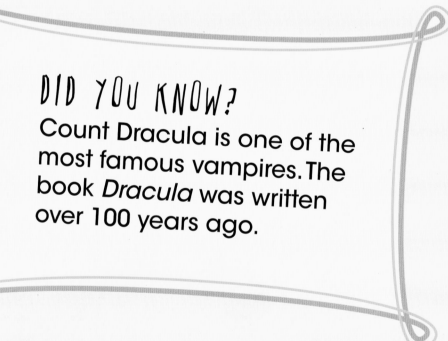

DID YOU KNOW?
Count Dracula is one of the most famous vampires. The book *Dracula* was written over 100 years ago.

Many stories tell of vampires who lie
in coffins or graveyards in the daytime.
They hunt for **victims** at night. They
bite people with **fangs** and suck
their blood.

DID YOU KNOW?
Some stories say
vampires don't have a
reflection or a shadow.

# The vampire myth

People all over the world tell stories about vampires. The **myths** may have started with real blood-sucking animals, such as vampire bats.

vampire bat

Yara-ma-yha-who

# DID YOU KNOW?

Australian **aboriginal** people have myths about Yara-ma-yha-who (say *yarra-ma-ya-hoo*). It is a small vampire that sucks blood from **victims** using suckers on its fingers.

# Vampires of Europe

There are many vampire **myths** in Eastern Europe. In Serbia a vampire called Sava Savanovic (say *sa-va sa-va-no-vitch*) was supposed to live in a **watermill**. Stories say he killed people who came to the mill and drank their blood.

Europe

Serbia

Romania

Greece

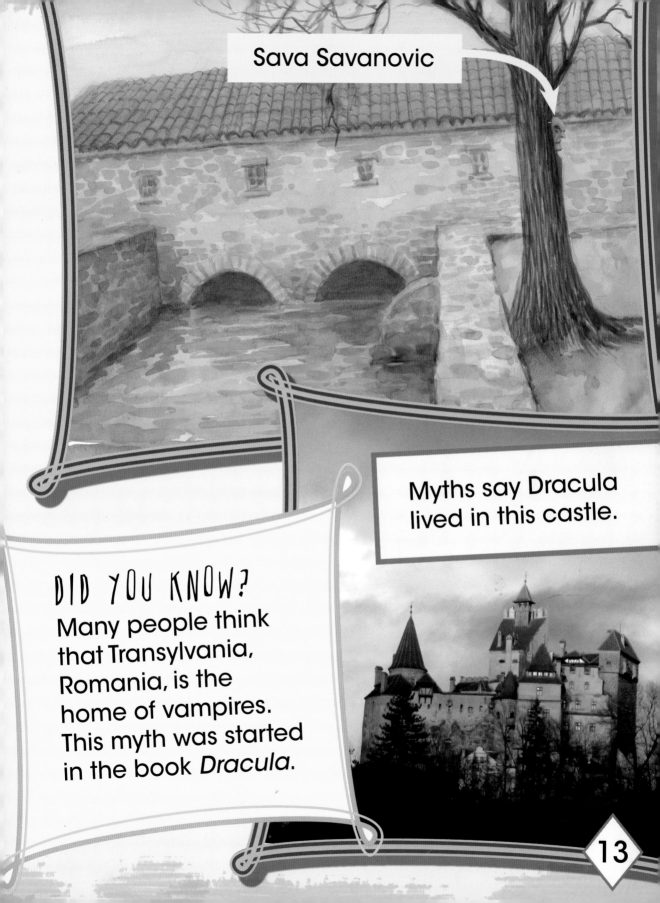

Sava Savanovic

Myths say Dracula lived in this castle.

**DID YOU KNOW?**
Many people think that Transylvania, Romania, is the home of vampires. This myth was started in the book *Dracula*.

wooden stake

crucifix

holy water

HOLY ✝ WATER

**Myths** from Europe say that a hawthorn branch or garlic keeps vampires away. A **crucifix** or holy water could also work. Myths say that putting a wooden **stake** through a vampire's heart kills it.

Lamia

# DID YOU KNOW?

Ancient Greek myths tell about a blood-sucking creature called Lamia (say *la-mee-ah*). She sucked children's blood at night.

15

# Vampires of Africa

There are many vampire **myths** in West Africa. The Adze (say *ad-zay*) was a vampire who turned into a firefly. It went into homes at night and sucked the blood of **victims**.

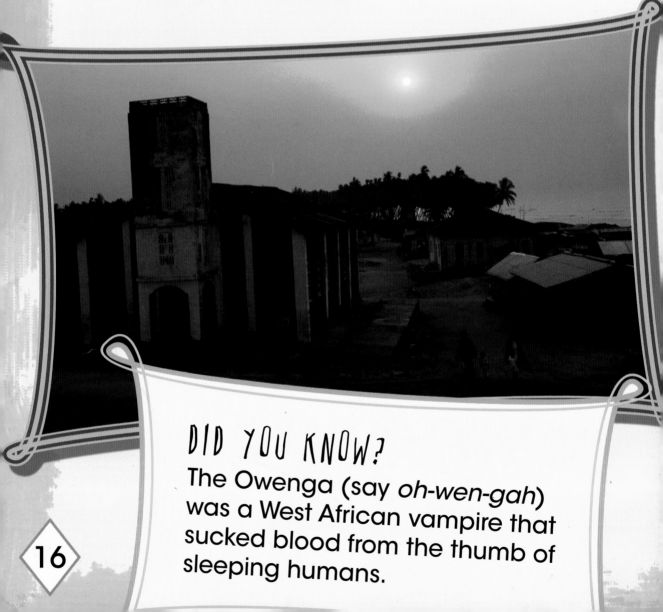

## DID YOU KNOW?

The Owenga (say *oh-wen-gah*) was a West African vampire that sucked blood from the thumb of sleeping humans.

This Makonde (say *mack-on-day*) vampire mask comes from Tanzania.

Africa

Tanzania

N

The Asanbosam (say *ah-san-bo-sam*) lived in West African forests. It had iron teeth and hooks on its feet. It used its hooks and claws to scoop **victims** up into the trees.

bells

DID YOU KNOW?
Some people in Africa kept
vampires away by:
• ringing small bells
• carving a post in their house.

# Vampires of Asia

Vampire **myths** are also told in Asia. In China the Jiang Shi (say *jee-ang shee*) was a dead body that killed people to get life from them. It had **mouldy** skin and long white hair.

woman dressed as a Jiang Shi

Asia

China→

Philippines→

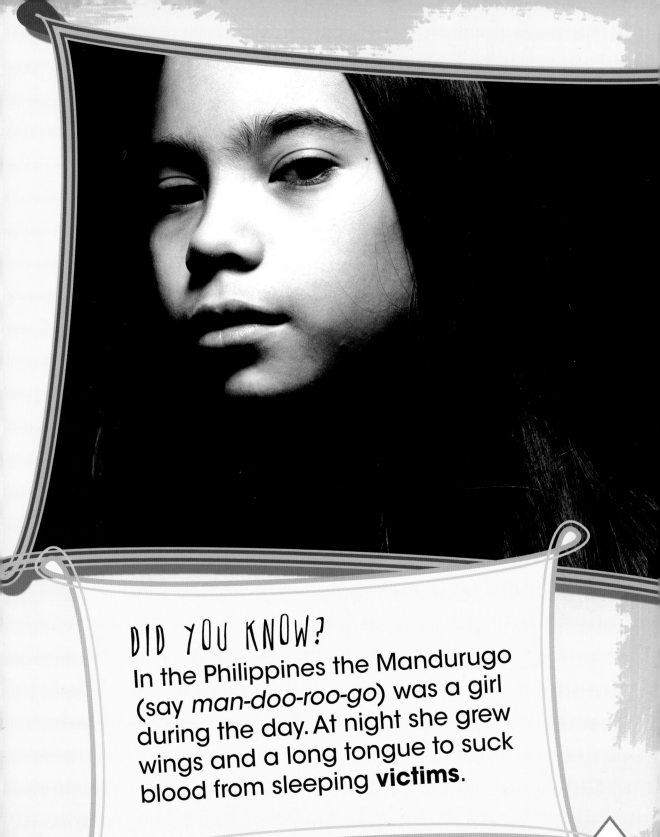

## DID YOU KNOW?

In the Philippines the Mandurugo (say *man-doo-roo-go*) was a girl during the day. At night she grew wings and a long tongue to suck blood from sleeping **victims**.

# Vampires of North and South America

In Colombia the Tunda (say *toon-dah*) was a female vampire who could **shape-shift**. She turned into a beautiful woman. Then she took men to the forest and sucked their blood.

North America
Mexico
Colombia
South America

The Nahuatl Indians
in Mexico believed
in vampires called
Tlaciques (say
*tuh-la-see-kways*).
These vampires were
witches who turned
into balls of flame.

# Close relatives

Other **mythical** creatures around the world are similar to vampires. The zombie is another **undead** creature. It is a dead body that has been brought back to life.

zombies

lightning bird

## DID YOU KNOW?

**Myths** say the African lightning bird **shape-shifts** to look like a man and then sucks **victims'** blood.

# Could vampires exist?

 **They could be real...**

- People all over the world tell stories about vampires.

 **I'm not so sure...**

- Stories can be made up. Many stories all over the world are similar.

 **They could be real...**

- Vampires live in coffins and dark places so we may not be able to see them.

 **I'm not so sure...**

- Vampire stories are just made up to scare people.

**They could be real...**

- Some things have really bitten people in their sleep and sucked their blood.

 **I'm not so sure...**

- People could have been bitten by a vampire bat or a biting insect.

There are many interesting stories about vampires. What do you think?

# Reality versus myth

## Vampire bat (real)

Found: Central and South America

Lives: caves, trees, old buildings

Eats: blood of birds and animals, sometimes humans

Special power: uses **echolocation** to find its way in the dark

Seen: with an **infrared** camera.

# Vampire (myth)

Found: all over the world

Lives: coffins, graveyards, forests

Eats: human blood

Special power: hard to kill

Seen: in films and books.

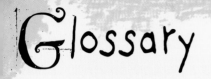
# Glossary

**aboriginal**  first people living in Australia

**crucifix**  model of a Christian cross

**echolocation**  using the sound of echoes to find the way

**fangs**  long, sharp teeth

**infrared**  special kind of light used to show things in the dark

**mouldy**  covered in a layer of fungus

**myth**  traditional story, often about magical creatures and events

**mythical**  found in myths

**shape-shift**  change the way someone or something looks

**stake**  pointed stick

**undead**  something that has died but is somehow still moving among the living

**victim**  person who is attacked

**watermill**  building with machinery to grind flour, powered by moving water

# Find out more

## Books

*Dracula*, retold by Mike Stocks
(Usborne Books, 2004)

*The Usborne Book of Myths and Legends*,
Gill Doherty (Usborne Publishing, 2006)

*Twilight*, Stephanie Meyer (Atom, 2007)

## Websites

**http://animals.nationalgeographic.com/
animals/mammals/common-vampire-bat.html**
Learn all about the vampire bat at this National
Geographic website.

**www.fieldmuseum.org/mythiccreatures/index.
html**
Learn about more mythical creatures at the Field
Museum's Mythic Creatures Exhibit website.

# Index